THE PHILADELPHIA FLYERS

BY
MARK STEWART

CONTENT CONSULTANT
DENIS GIBBONS
SOCIETY FOR INTERNATIONAL HOCKEY RESEARCH

NORWOOD HOUSE PRESS
CHICAGO, ILLINOIS

Norwood House Press
P.O. Box 316598
Chicago, Illinois 60631

For information regarding Norwood House Press, please visit our website at:
www.norwoodhousepress.com or call 866-565-2900.

All photos courtesy of Associated Press except the following:
Topps, Inc. (6, 15, 16, 42 both), Hockey Hall of Fame (7, 8, 9, 40, 41), Quarton Group/NHL (10),
Author's Collection (21, 33, 43 bottom), Beckett Publications (23, 38), Black Book Partners (25, 27, 34),
Prentice-Hall (31), Tiger Press, Inc. (35 top left, 43 top), TIME Inc./Sports Illustrated for Kids (35 top right),
Summit Books (37), O-Pee-Chee Ltd. (45).
Cover Photo: Cal Sport Media via AP Images

The memorabilia and artifacts pictured in this book are presented for educational and informational purposes,
and come from the collection of the author.

Editor: Mike Kennedy
Designer: Ron Jaffe
Project Management: Black Book Partners, LLC.
Special thanks to Topps, Inc.

Library of Congress Cataloging-in-Publication Data

Stewart, Mark, 1960 July 7-
    The Philadelphia Flyers / by Mark Stewart.
        pages cm. -- (Team spirit)
    Includes bibliographical references and index.
    Summary: "A revised Team Spirit Hockey edition featuring the Philadelphia
Flyers that chronicles the history and accomplishments of the team. Includes
access to the Team Spirit website which provides additional information and
photos"-- Provided by publisher.
    ISBN 978-1-59953-625-5 (library edition : alk. paper) -- ISBN
978-1-60357-633-8 (ebook) 1. Philadelphia Flyers (Hockey
Team)--History--Juvenile literature. I. Title.
    GV848.P48S74 2014
    796.962'640974811--dc23
                                                                2013030876

Manufactured in the United States of America in Stevens Point, Wisconsin.
239N—012014

COVER PHOTO: Two members of the Flyers congratulate each other after a victory.

TABLE OF CONTENTS

ABOUT OUR GLOSSARY

In this book, there may be several words that you are reading for the first time. Some are sports words, some are new vocabulary words, and some are familiar words that are used in an unusual way. All of these words are defined on page 46. Throughout the book, sports words appear in **bold type**. Regular vocabulary words appear in *bold italic type*.

The personality of most hockey teams changes from season to season. Some years a team has a powerful offense, and other years it has a tight defense. Sometimes a great coach leads the way, and other times it's an amazing goalie. The Philadelphia Flyers have a funny way of putting the same kind of team on the ice year after year. The Flyers value size, strength, teamwork, and unselfish play.

Remarkable things can happen when a team is built this way. Everyday players find ways to raise their games. Stars do the little things that lead to victory. And in the stands, the fans cheer with enormous pride and pleasure.

This book tells the story of the Flyers. They are a tough, hardworking team in a tough, hardworking city. Players may come to the Flyers from all over the world, but when their careers are over, they definitely take a little "Philly" attitude with them.

Kimmo Timonen and Claude Giroux talk strategy after a goal during the 2012–13 season.

GLORY DAYS

ED VAN IMPE
DEFENSE

uring the 1950s and 1960s, the **National Hockey League (NHL)** found success by keeping things small. Only six teams competed for the **Stanley Cup** each season. In the mid-1960s, the league decided it was time to expand. The NHL added six new clubs, all in the United States—two in the west, one in the north, one in the midwest, and two in Pennsylvania, the Pittsburgh Penguins and the Flyers. To stock the new teams, the NHL held a special **draft**.

With their first two picks, the Flyers took Bernie Parent and Doug Favell, both young goaltenders. Philadelphia also added Ed Van Impe, who was runner-up for **Rookie** of the Year a season earlier, and another defensemen, Joe Watson. Also coming to the team in the draft was Gary Dornhoefer and Lou Angotti, an experienced center who would be named the team's first captain.

To create excitement for fans, the NHL grouped all the new teams together in the West **Division**. That meant that an **expansion team** was guaranteed to make it to the **Stanley Cup Finals**. For most of the 1967–68 season, the Flyers looked like the best bet

to compete for the championship. Favell and Parent were excellent in goal, while Angotti led the club in scoring. Philadelphia finished in first place but lost in the **playoffs**. The Flyers bowed out in the first round the following season, too. Both times, they were beaten by a more physical opponent.

Ed Snider, the Flyers' owner, became frustrated. He vowed that he would build a team that no one would push around. In the first round of the 1969 draft, Philadelphia selected Bobby Clarke. He fit Snider's plan perfectly. Clarke was a physical defender who was not scared of a hard **check**. He was also an expert at taking **faceoffs**. Clarke teamed with Bill Barber and Bill Flett. This trio helped the Flyers win their first Stanley Cup, in 1973–74. It marked the first time an expansion club had won the NHL title.

LEFT: Ed Van Impe was one of Philadelphia's first stars.
ABOVE: Bernie Parent slides to his right to make a save.

The following season, the Flyers replaced Flett on Clarke's **line** with Reggie Leach. The two had played **junior hockey** together and were a great one-two punch. The result was better than the team could have dreamed. The Flyers won another championship that spring and then reached the Stanley Cup Finals for the third time in a row in 1975–76. In all, the LCB Line (L for Leach, C for Clarke, and B for Barber) would play together for nine seasons.

Just as their owner had planned, the Flyers won their two Stanley Cups with a combination of skill and *intimidation*. The NHL did not discourage violence and fighting during the 1970s, and Philadelphia took advantage. The Flyers were known as the "Broad Street Bullies," daring opponents to trade punches with them. Dave Schultz, Bob Kelly, Don Saleski, and Andre DuPont were the biggest and toughest of the Flyers, but just about every player on the team was willing to "drop the gloves."

The Flyers returned to the Stanley Cup Finals three times during the 1980s. The scoring stars of these teams included Terry Crisp,

LEFT: Bobby Clarke and Bill Barber teamed up on the same line for more than 10 years.   **ABOVE**: Reggie Leach combined with Clarke and Barber on the famous LCB line.

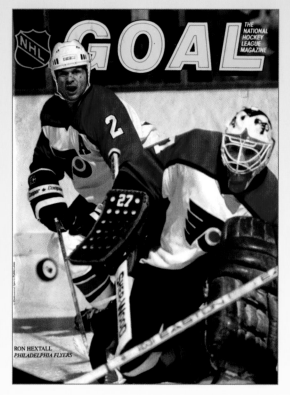

RON HEXTALL
PHILADELPHIA FLYERS

Tim Kerr, Peter Zezel, Brian Propp, Dave Poulin, Ilkka Sinisalo, and Rick Tocchet. The defense was anchored by Mark Howe, the son of all-time great Gordie Howe. The Flyers also had several talented goalies during this period, including Pete Peeters, Pelle Lindbergh, and Ron Hextall. Lindbergh had one of the greatest seasons ever in 1984–85 at the age of 25. A year later, he died in a car accident. Hextall played 11 years for the team and became a fan favorite because of his *aggressive* play.

In the late 1980s and early 1990s, the Flyers had several poor seasons in a row. They saw a chance to turn things around in 1992, when teenager Eric Lindros announced that he did not care to play for the Quebec Nordiques, the team that had just drafted him. The Flyers made a bold trade to get Lindros, who was considered the best young player of his *generation*. Lindros centered for a line that included big John LeClair and Mikael Renberg. The trio's nickname was "The Legion of Doom." They led the Flyers to the **conference** finals in the 1994–95 season and all the way to the Stanley Cup Finals two years later.

From 1994–95 through 2012–13, the Flyers had a winning record in every year but one. During that time, they finished first in their division six times and returned to the Stanley Cup Finals in 2010. They fell short of a third championship in that series, losing to the Chicago Blackhawks.

Like the Flyers of old, the team today continues to win with a combination of toughness and talent. In recent years, some of Philadelphia's best players have been "homegrown," including Claude Giroux, Mike Richards, Simon Gagne, and Jeff Carter. Others have been plucked from the rosters of competing teams, such as Scott Hartnell, Wayne Simmonds, Ilya Bryzgalov, Danny Briere, and Chris Pronger. What they share is a dedication to the game, a hunger for victory, and the intense pride that comes with being a Flyer.

LEFT: This magazine cover features Mark Howe and Ron Hextall.
ABOVE: Ilya Bryzgalov and Wayne Simmonds celebrate a big victory.

HOME ICE

The Flyers played their first 30 seasons in an arena called The Spectrum. It was Philadelphia's first modern sports arena. In 1996, the team moved into its current home. Many fans call it "The Spectrum II." The arena is also home to the 76ers basketball team.

The Flyers' arena is one of the largest in the NHL. When the team sells standing-room tickets, attendance is more than 20,000. The arena features a modern video scoreboard, and both Stanley Cup banners hang from the ceiling—along with the team's retired jerseys. Lou Nolan, the arena's announcer, has seen it all there. Nolan started working games for the Flyers in 1972, and he was still behind the microphone in 2013.

BY THE NUMBERS

- The Flyers' arena has 19,537 seats for hockey.
- The arena hosted the *X Games* twice, in 2001 and 2002.
- As of 2013, the Flyers had retired five numbers: 1 (Bernie Parent), 2 (Mark Howe), 4 (Barry Ashbee), 7 (Bill Barber), and 16 (Bobby Clarke).

A camera located inside the goal provides a nice view of the Flyers' arena.

DRESSED FOR SUCCESS

The Flyers got their name from the team's first *general manager*, Bud Poile. He had once run a club in the **minor leagues** called the Flyers. Poile liked the name, and so did the team owners. Philadelphia has used the same *logo* and colors since the team's first NHL season. Their uniform combines orange, black, and white. The logo is the letter *P* made to look like a wing.

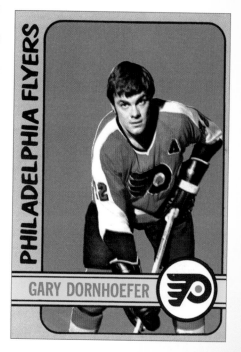

In 1981–82, the Flyers experimented with long pants that were supposed to help the players skate faster. Fans didn't like the look, and the Flyers stopped the experiment—but not because of the public reaction. When players fell to the ice, the long pants made it impossible for them to stop sliding!

PHILADELPHIA FLYERS

GARY DORNHOEFER

LEFT: Jakub Voracek wears the Flyers' home uniform in 2012–13.
ABOVE: As this trading card of Gary Dornhoefer shows, the team used a darker shade of orange in its early years.

WE WON!

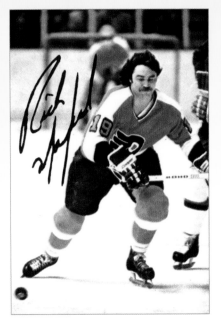

The Flyers made it to the Stanley Cup Finals six times in their first 43 seasons. On four of those occasions, the year ended in disappointment for Philadelphia fans. However, no loss can ever cast a shadow over the back-to-back championships the team won in the 1970s. In the 100-plus years that sports teams have been playing in Philadelphia, no group of players was as beloved as the Flyers of this era.

When the 1973–74 season began, the Flyers had just one winning year in their history. Coach Fred Shero was determined to change that. He had an important player back in Philadelphia to help him. Bernie Parent had been traded to the Toronto Maple Leafs in 1971. Parent returned two years later and was better than ever. He won 47 games, and his 1.89 goals-against average led the league. Three of Parent's teammates joined him in

the NHL **All-Star Game** that winter: center Bobby Clarke and defensemen Joe Watson and Ed Van Impe.

Come playoff time, Clarke and Rick MacLeish led the offense. The Flyers swept the Atlanta Flames in the opening round, and then survived a seven-game series with the New York Rangers in the conference finals. Gary Dornhoefer netted the winning goal in Game 7 midway through the third period.

In the Stanley Cup Finals against the Boston Bruins, the Flyers lost the first game on the road. But Clarke scored in overtime to win Game 2. That victory fired up the Flyers as the series moved home

LEFT: As this card shows, high-scoring Rick MacLeish was never far from a loose puck.   **ABOVE**: The Flyers celebrate a goal in their series against the Boston Bruins.

to Philadelphia. Parent was sensational in goal, and Philadelphia took the series in six games. In the decisive contest, MacLeish scored a goal in the first period, and Parent and the defense made it stand up for a 1–0 victory. The parade that followed in Philadelphia was like no celebration in city history. Schools and businesses closed down, and police estimated that there were more people lining the streets than the actual population of Philadelphia!

The cast of characters for the 1974–75 season barely changed from the year before. Clarke had a spectacular season and won the Hart Trophy as league Most Valuable Player (MVP). Parent won 44 games and had 12 **shutouts** for the second season in a row. Newcomer Reggie Leach topped the club with 45 goals. Dave Schultz, the team's primary **enforcer**, set a record with 472 penalty minutes—an average of more than six per game.

The road to the Stanley Cup Finals was similar to the year before. Philadelphia swept its first-round opponent, the Maple Leafs. Then they faced another seven-game struggle against another New York team, the Islanders. The recipe for success stayed the same. The Flyers wore down their opponents with physical play, Clarke and MacLeish led a quick-striking offense, and Parent was superb in goal.

The Flyers faced the Buffalo Sabres for the Stanley Cup. The two teams split the first four games, each winning on their home

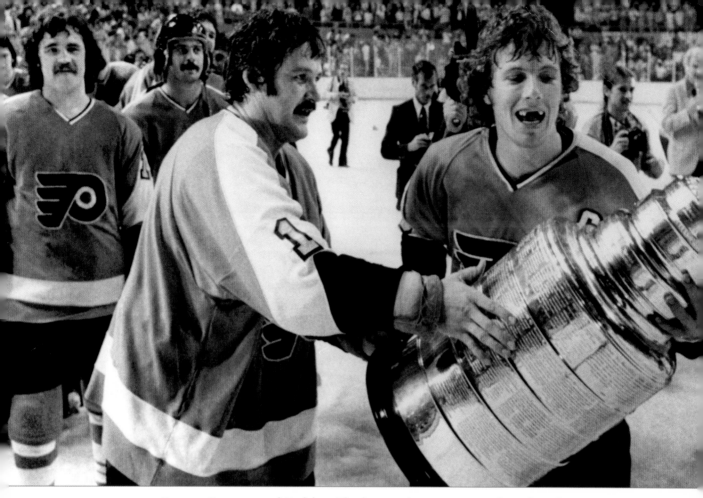

Bernie Parent and Bobby Clarke can't wait to get their hands
on the Stanley Cup in 1975.

ice. Game 3 was played with thick fog hovering over the ice. There was
a heat wave in Buffalo, and the Sabres' arena did not have a good air
conditioning system. The cold ice and warm, humid air created a small
weather front that stopped play several times. The Flyers won the final
two games, however, to take the series. Parent was awarded the Conn
Smythe Trophy for the second year in a row as the MVP of the playoffs.

GO-TO GUYS

To be a true star in the NHL, you need more than a great slapshot. You have to be a "go-to guy"—someone teammates trust to make the winning play when the seconds are ticking away in a big game. Flyers fans have had a lot to cheer about over the years, including these great stars.

THE PIONEERS

BERNIE PARENT   Goalie

- BORN 4/3/1945
- PLAYED FOR TEAM: 1967–68 TO 1970–71 & 1973–74 TO 1978–79

Bernie Parent's amazing play in the 1974 and 1975 Stanley Cup Finals made him one of the most beloved athletes in Philadelphia history. His career ended with a weird injury. The edge of a stick went into the tiny eye slit of his goalie's mask and permanently damaged his vision.

BOBBY CLARKE   Center

- BORN 8/13/ 1949   • PLAYED FOR TEAM: 1969–70 TO 1983–84

Bobby Clarke was a tremendous all-around player. He understood what was needed to make a difference in any given game. It might be a great pass, a bone-crunching check, or a sizzling slapshot—but he always seemed to make the winning play.

BILL BARBER Left Wing

- BORN 7/11/1952   • PLAYED FOR TEAM: 1972–73 TO 1983–84

Bill Barber joined the Flyers at age 20, after just 11 minor-league games. He quickly became one of the NHL's top left wings—and an important team leader. In 2000–01, as Philadelphia's coach, Barber won the Jack Adams Award as coach of the year.

BRIAN PROPP Left Wing

- BORN 2/15/1959

- PLAYED FOR TEAM: 1979–80 TO 1989–90

The Flyers specialized in finding great left wings, and Brian Propp was among the very best. He topped 40 goals four times for Philadelphia and helped the team reach the Stanley Cup Finals three times.

MARK HOWE Defenseman

- BORN 5/28/1955

- PLAYED FOR TEAM: 1982–83 TO 1991–92

Mark Howe began his career in the **World Hockey Association (WHA)**, where he played forward alongside his father, Gordie, and brother, Marty. He switched to defense and helped the Flyers become one of the best defensive teams of the 1980s. Howe's skating and passing were also important weapons for the Philadelphia offense.

ABOVE: Brian Propp's intense focus is obvious in this signed photo.

RON HEXTALL — Goalie

- Born 5/3/1964
- Played for Team: 1986–87 to 1991–92
  & 1994–5 to 1998–99

Ron Hextall was like an extra defenseman on the ice. He loved to handle the puck and even checked opponents from time to time. As a rookie in 1986–87, Hextall won the Vezina Trophy as the league's best goalie and also the Conn Smythe Trophy—even though the Flyers lost the Stanley Cup to the Edmonton Oilers.

ROD BRIND'AMOUR — Center

- Born 8/9/1970 • Played for Team: 1991–92 to 1999–00

Few NHL centers were better than Rod Brind'Amour in the defensive end of the ice. If an opponent needed to be "shut down," he usually got the assignment. Brind'Amour was popular with fans and teammates—and most seasons he was among the team leaders in scoring.

ERIC LINDROS — Center

- Born 2/28/1973 • Played for Team: 1992–93 to 1999–2000

The Flyers got Eric Lindros in one of the most famous trades in NHL history. He led the team to the Stanley Cup Finals and won a Hart Trophy, but his career was sadly cut short. Despite wearing a helmet, Lindros suffered six *concussions* in his final three seasons with the Flyers.

ERIC DESJARDINS   Defenseman

- BORN 6/14/1969   • PLAYED FOR TEAM: 1994–95 TO 2005–06

The Flyers got Eric Desjardins and John LeClair in the same trade with the Montreal Canadiens. It proved to be one of the best deals that the team ever made. Desjardins was Philadelphia's defensive leader for 10 seasons.

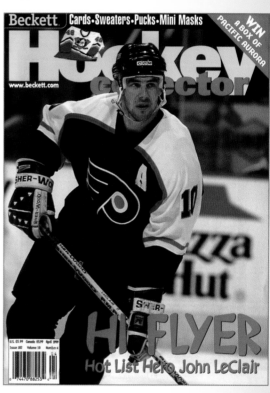

JOHN LeCLAIR   Left Wing

- BORN 7/5/1969

- PLAYED FOR TEAM: 1994–95 TO 2003–04

John LeClair combined size, speed, and stickwork as well as anyone in team history. He scored 50 or more goals in each of his first three full seasons in Philadelphia. LeClair was the first American-born player to reach this mark in back-to-back seasons.

CLAUDE GIROUX   Center

- BORN 1/12/1988

- FIRST SEASON WITH TEAM: 2007–08

The Flyers have always given young players a chance to prove themselves. Claude Giroux made the most of his opportunity. He led the team in scoring for three straight seasons from 2010–11 and 2012–13, and was later named team captain. Giroux battled back from an injury in 2012–13 and showed he was one of the best young players in the league.

LEFT: Ron Hextall was one of the few goalies who liked physical play.
RIGHT: John LeClair's   cards   re among the hottest in the hobby during the 1990s.

CALLING THE SHOTS

The Flyers have had some of the sport's top coaches during their history, including Pat Quinn, Mike Keenan, Roger Neilson, Bill Barber, Ken Hitchcock, and Peter Laviolette. Three of them—Quinn, Keenan, and Barber—earned the Jack Adams Award. Quinn was a genius when it came to finding small advantages for his team. He led the club to the Stanley Cup Finals in 1980. Keenan was known as "Iron Mike" because he could be extremely tough on his players. The Flyers reached the Stanley Cup Finals twice during his four seasons in Philadelphia. Barber, a former All-Star, coached the Flyers to a winning record in each of the two seasons he was behind the bench.

Fred Shero was by far the most successful coach for the Flyers. Shero was a player during the 1940s and 1950s, and he learned that teams could train—*and be trained*—much better if certain changes were made. He tested these ideas as a minor-league coach, and then continued to perfect them with the Flyers during the 1970s. For example, Shero put his players on weight-lifting programs so they

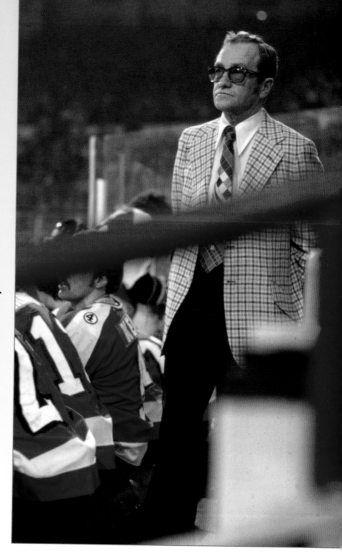

Fred Shero watches the action from the Flyers' bench.

could maintain their strength throughout the season.

Shero also took advantage of watching videotape, which was a *revolutionary* idea when he coached. He studied his own players as well as his opponents. In practice, Shero created playing systems for offense and defense, so he could call plays during games. He believed that two coaches were necessary to deal with all of these duties, so he chose to name an official assistant coach. Now every team has one.

Shero led the Flyers to two Stanley Cups. His players loved him. He seemed to know exactly what to say to *inspire* the Flyers and how to keep them focused. Shero was elected to the **Hall of Fame** in 2013.

MAY 19, 1974

The 1974 Stanley Cup Finals pitted the Flyers against the Boston Bruins. Philadelphia was hockey's toughest team, and Boston was the game's most talented. During the regular season, the Bruins had the NHL's four top scorers. Phil Esposito led the league with 68 goals, Bobby Orr led the league with 90 **assists**, Ken Hodge netted 50 goals, and Wayne Cashman finished fourth behind his three teammates with 89 points (goals plus assists)—two ahead of Bobby Clarke.

Given Boston's high-scoring offense, Philadelphia coach Fred Shero knew he had to change *strategies*. His Broad Street Bullies would be unable to push the Bruins around. The Flyers would have to find another way to win.

Most teams tried their best to keep the puck away from Orr when they played the Bruins. Shero ordered his players to do the opposite. Time and again, the Flyers dumped the puck into Orr's part of rink, forcing him to skate back and start each play. The constant pressure

Bobby Clarke wears the captain's C against the Boston Bruins.

wore down the All-Star defenseman. As Orr tired, Philadelphia seized the edge in the series.

During a heart-pounding Game 6 in Philadelphia, Orr and his teammates threw everything they had at the Flyers. Goalie Bernie Parent came under constant attack, but he turned back every shot. With five minutes left in the opening period, defenseman Andre DuPont snapped a shot toward the Boston goal. Rick MacLeish redirected the puck with the blade of his stick past Gilles Gilbert, and the Flyers went ahead 1–0.

Over the next two periods, the two teams hammered away at each other. Neither goalie allowed another score. Parent turned back a total of 30 shots. As the final seconds ticked away, Philadelphia announcer Gene Hart shouted, "Ladies and gentlemen, the Flyers are going to win the Stanley Cup ... the Flyers win the Stanley Cup! The Flyers win the Stanley Cup!"

LEGEND HAS IT

WAS THE 2009–10 SHOOTOUT AGAINST THE NEW YORK RANGERS THE GREATEST IN NHL HISTORY?

LEGEND HAS IT that it was. On the last day of the season, the Flyers and Rangers played for their conference's final

playoff spot. The game was tied 1–1 after three periods and an overtime. Danny Briere and Claude Giroux scored **shootout** goals for the Flyers to put them up 2–1. Olli Jokinen took the last shot for the Rangers. Brian Boucher stopped it, sending the Flyers to the **postseason**—where they made it all the way to the Stanley Cup Finals!

ABOVE: Brian Boucher makes the decisive save in the shootout against the New York Rangers.

WHO WAS THE NHL'S MOST FAMOUS GOOD LUCK CHARM?

LEGEND HAS IT that Kate Smith was. During the 1940s, Smith was one of America's most popular singers. During the early 1970s, the Flyers often played her version of "God Bless America" at their home games. When they did, they were nearly unbeatable. For Game 6 of the 1974 Stanley Cup Finals, the team flew the 67-year-old Smith to Philadelphia to perform the song live. Phil Esposito of the Boston Bruins tried to "jinx" Smith by presenting her with a bouquet of roses, but the Flyers won 1–0 to capture the Cup.

WHICH NHL GOALIE WAS THE FIRST TO BRING A WATER BOTTLE TO HIS POSITION?

LEGEND HAS IT that Bob Froese was. During the 1984–85 season, Froese decided to copy what he'd seen in college games and bring a supply of water with him onto the ice. Soon teammate Pelle Lindbergh did the same. They kept their bottles on top of the net, securing them with strips of velcro. No league rules were broken, but some opposing teams were annoyed. After one game, coach Glen Sather of the Edmonton Oilers complained, "What are they going to want up there next … a bucket of chicken?"

When the 1975 Stanley Cup Finals began, some experts predicted the Buffalo Sabres would need a miracle to beat the Flyers. They actually got one in Game 3 of the series. Referees had to stop the action again and again during the contest at Buffalo's Memorial Auditorium. The problem was that no one could see.

A swirling fog bank that looked like a witch's cauldron kept forming over the playing surface. Fans couldn't see the players, players couldn't see the puck, and the referees had no idea what was going on. Each time the refs whistled for the action to stop, players from both teams were asked to skate in circles to make the fog go away. Each time play restarted, the fog would come back. And just when things seemed like they couldn't get any stranger, a *disoriented* bat flew out of the rafters and crashed onto the ice!

Meanwhile, the Flyers and Sabres squared off in a close, exciting game. Philadelphia led 4–3, but the Sabres tied the score to force overtime. Conditions only got worse. The game was stopped seven times in the extra period. With less than a minute left, Buffalo's

Bernie Parent once said he could write a book about his strange life in hockey … so he did!

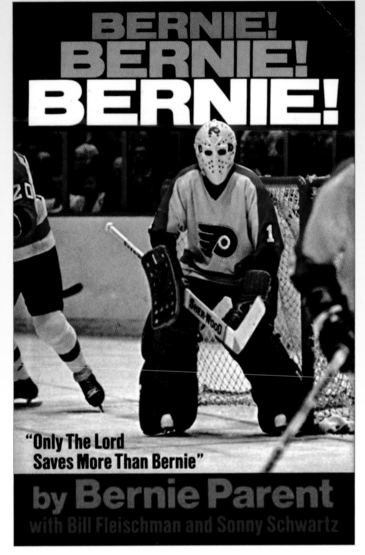

Rene Robert flicked a shot from the right side at Bernie Parent. The Flyers' goalie never saw the puck, which went right between his legs to win the game. Fortunately for Philadelphia, the team regrouped to win the series.

No one is really sure what caused the fog bank in Buffalo. The air that day was warm and humid, and the arena did not have a good air conditioning system. All Parent remembers was the goal he never saw. Later, he joked that he wouldn't have taken his boat out in those conditions … much less try to play a hockey game!

P hiladelphia was known as the "City of Brotherly Love" long before the Flyers came to town. But Flyers fans have treated their players like beloved brothers since their first season. They take enormous pride in the team's victories. They also take losses very hard.

Hockey players appreciate this kind of devotion. Indeed, dozens of former Flyers have chosen to live in the area after they retired.

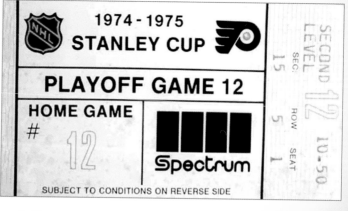

Most NHL teams see their attendance rise and fall based on wins and losses. The Flyers are different. Their fans fill the building no matter how the club is doing. In seasons when Philadelphia misses the playoffs, ticket sales during the regular season are still very strong. In years when the Flyers are fighting for first place, finding a ticket to a game is just about impossible!

LEFT: Sean Couturier greets young fans before a game. The Flyers have a very close bond with their fans.
ABOVE: For Philly fans, old ticket stubs like this one are like gold.

TIMELINE

The hockey season is played from October through June. That means each season takes place at the end of one year and the beginning of the next. In this timeline, the accomplishments of the Flyers are shown by season.

1972–73
Rick MacLeish scores 50 goals.

1975–76
Bobby Clarke wins his third Hart Trophy.

1967–68
The Flyers finish atop the West Division in their first season.

1973–74
The Flyers win their first of two straight Stanley Cups.

1979–80
Reggie Leach is the All-Star Game MVP.

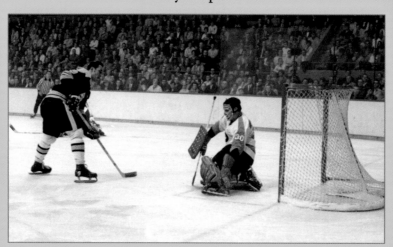

Bernie Parent makes a save in the Flyers' first season.

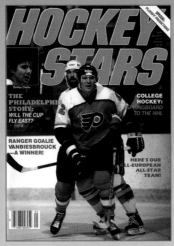

Tim Kerr

Eric Lindros

1985–86

Tim Kerr scores a record 34 goals on the **power play**.

1991–92

The Flyers trade for Eric Lindros.

1996–97

The Flyers reach the Stanley Cup Finals for the fifth time.

1986–87

The Flyers record their third 100-point season in a row.

1992–93

Mark Recchi sets a team record with 123 points.

2011–12

Claude Giroux sets a team record with six points in a playoff game.

Claude Giroux celebrates with Maxime Talbot during his record-setting game.

FUN FACTS

HE SHOOTS ... HE SCORES!

Many NHL goalies dream of firing the puck down the ice, past all six opponents, and into the other goal. The first to do so was Ron Hextall. As a rookie, he scored against the Boston Bruins after they had pulled their own goalie off the ice for an extra skater.

DOIN' THE BERNIE

Prior to the 1980s, only one goalie in history had his number retired by an NHL club. In 1979, the Flyers announced that no Philadelphia player would ever wear Bernie Parent's number 1 again.

UNDEFEATED

During the 1979–80 season, the Flyers went from October 14 to January 6 without losing a game. They won 25 games and tied 10. Their 35-game unbeaten streak set a record for American *professional* team sports.

It wasn't hard for Dave Schultz to pick the title of his book.

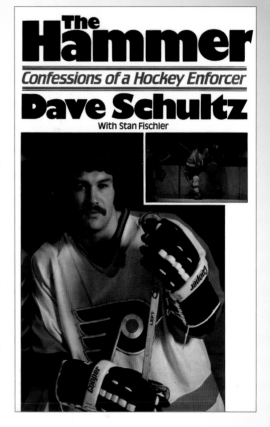

HAMMER TIME

Of all the Broad Street Bullies in the 1970s, there was no bigger bully than Dave "The Hammer" Schultz. Roughly one in five penalties called on the team resulted in Schultz taking a trip to the penalty box. In 1974–75, he had 472 penalty minutes. That mark still stands as a league record.

GUFFAW!

When Brian Propp scored goals for the Flyers, he would skate to center ice, raise his arm and shout "Guffaw!" He got the idea from comedian Howie Mandel, who used it as part of his act.

DOING IT THE HARD WAY

In 1979–80, Reggie Leach scored 50 goals. Only five came on the power play; the other 45 were scored at even strength. No 50-goal scorer has ever had so few power-play goals.

TALKING HOCKEY

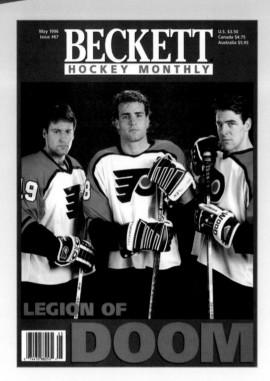

May 1996
Issue #67

BECKETT
HOCKEY MONTHLY

U.S. $3.50
Canada $4.75
Australia $5.95

LEGION OF
DOOM

"It was a great feeling playing with those two guys. Every time you went on the ice you felt like something was going to happen."

▶ **JOHN LECLAIR**, *on Eric Lindros, Mikael Renberg, and the Legion of Doom line*

"We take the shortest route to the puck and arrive in ***ill humor***."

▶ **BOBBY CLARKE**, *on how his teams combined speed and toughness*

"It's not necessarily the amount of time you spend at practice that counts; it's what you put into the practice."

▶ **ERIC LINDROS**, *on the importance of working at your game*

"He was as dedicated an athlete as I have ever worked with."

▶ **MIKE KEENAN**, *on the work ethic of Tim Kerr*

"G's probably the biggest competitor that I have ever played with. He wants to win so badly."

▶ **SCOTT HARTNELL**, *on Claude Giroux*

"As a Flyer, you play for the emblem on the front, not the name on the back."

▶ **FRED SHERO**, *on Philadelphia's team spirit*

"You don't have to be crazy to be a goalie. But it helps!"

▶ **BERNIE PARENT**, *on what made him a top netminder*

LEFT: Mikael Renberg, Eric Lindros, and John LeClair—also known as The Legion of Doom!   **ABOVE**: Scott Hartnell and Claude Giroux

GREAT DEBATES

People who root for the Flyers love to compare their favorite moments, teams, and players. Some debates have been going on for years! How would you settle these classic hockey arguments?

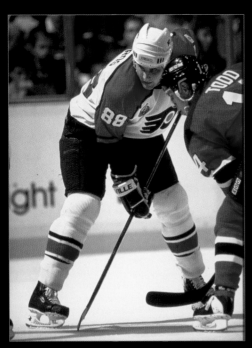

THE 1992 TRADE FOR ERIC LINDROS WAS A GOOD ONE ...

... because it pumped new life into the Flyers. The team had missed the playoffs three years in a row. With Lindros (**LEFT**) leading the way, Philadelphia finished first or second six years in a row and made it to the Stanley Cup Finals in 1997. Lindros was the most exciting young player in hockey. How would Flyers fans have felt if a rival team like the Rangers got him?

THE TEAM WOULD HAVE BEEN FINE WITHOUT LINDROS ...

... because many of the players Philadelphia gave up in the trade turned out to be very good. Peter Forsberg, Mike Ricci, Chris Simon, and Steve Duchesne would have helped the team get to the playoffs, too. And the draft picks the Flyers gave up might have helped them win the Stanley Cup, not just reach the finals.

THE BROAD STREET BULLIES WERE BAD FOR THE NHL ...

... because they popularized fighting and violence. A certain amount of hard contact is normal in a hockey game. But the Flyers of the 1970s used their elbows and fists to win games by drawing opponents into fights and terrorizing their star players. Those Philadelphia teams had great talent—they could have won without all the bullying.

NONSENSE. THE FLYERS HELPED MAKE HOCKEY A PRIMETIME SPORT ...

... because, love them or hate them, sports fans wanted to see the Broad Street Bullies play. True, many opponents dreaded their games with the Flyers. But Philadelphia won championships with smart team play, tough defense, and great goaltending. Besides, if they made  fighting so glamorous, how come there is so little fighting in the NHL today?

FOR THE RECORD

T he great Flyers teams and players have left their marks on the record books. These are the "best of the best" ...

ALL ★ STAR

PELLE LINDBERGH G

Pelle Lindbergh

FLYERS

BILL BARBER

Bill Barber

FLYERS AWARD WINNERS

HART MEMORIAL TROPHY
MOST VALUABLE PLAYER

Bobby Clarke	1972–73
Bobby Clarke	1974–75
Bobby Clarke	1975–76
Eric Lindros	1994–95

LESTER B. PEARSON AWARD
MOST OUTSTANDING PLAYER

Bobby Clarke	1972–73
Eric Lindros	1994–95

CONN SMYTHE TROPHY
MVP DURING PLAYOFFS

Bernie Parent	1973–74
Bernie Parent	1974–75
Reggie Leach	1975–76
Ron Hextall	1986–87

FRANK J. SELKE TROPHY
TOP DEFENSIVE FORWARD

Bobby Clarke	1982–83
Dave Poulin	1986–87

JACK ADAMS AWARD
COACH OF THE YEAR

Fred Shero	1973–74
Pat Quinn	1979–80
Mike Keenan	1984–85
Bill Barber	2000–01

ALL-STAR GAME MVP

Reggie Leach	1979–80

VEZINA TROPHY
TOP GOALTENDER

Bernie Parent	1973–74
Bernie Parent	1974–75
Pelle Lindbergh	1984–85
Ron Hextall	1986–87

WILLIAM JENNINGS TROPHY
GOALTENDER WITH FEWEST GOALS ALLOWED

Bob Froese & Darren Jensen	1985–86
Roman Cechmanek & Robert Esche	2002–03

FLYERS ACHIEVEMENTS

ACHIEVEMENT	YEAR
Campbell Conference Champions	1973–74
Stanley Cup Champions	1973–74
Campbell Conference Champions	1974–75
Stanley Cup Champions	1974–75
Campbell Conference Champions	1975–76
Campbell Conference Champions	1979–80
Wales Conference Champions	1984–85
Wales Conference Champions	1986–87
Eastern Conference Champions	1996–97
Eastern Conference Champions	2009–10

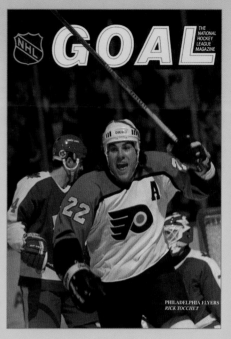

Rick Tocchet was a star for the great teams of the 1980s.

Oops! The Flyers made this pennant thinking they would win the Stanley Cup in 1987. Instead, they lost to the Edmonton Oilers.

PINPOINTS

The history of a hockey team is made up of many smaller stories. These stories take place all over the map—not just in the city a team calls "home." Match the pushpins on these maps to the **TEAM FACTS**, and you will begin to see the story of the Flyers unfold!

1 Philadelphia, Pennsylvania—*The Flyers have played here since 1967.*

2 Detroit, Michigan—*Mark Howe was born here.*

3 St. Albans, Vermont—*John LeClair was born here.*

4 Buffalo, New York—*The Flyers won the 1975 Stanley Cup here.*

5 Phoenix, Arizona—*Sean Couturier was born here.*

6 Flin Flon, Manitoba—*Bobby Clarke was born here.*

7 Montreal, Quebec—*Bernie Parent was born here.*

8 Callander, Ontario—*Bill Barber was born here.*

9 Saskatoon, Saskatchewan—*Ed Van Impe was born here.*

10 Smithers, British Columbia—*Joe Watson was born here.*

11 Stockholm, Sweden—*Pelle Lindbergh was born here.*

12 Valkeakoski, Finland—*Ilkka Sinisalo was born here.*

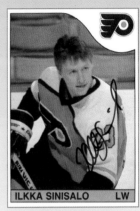

ILKKA SINISALO   LW

Ilkka Sinisalo

45

GLOSSARY

HOCKEY WORDS
VOCABULARY WORDS

AGGRESSIVE—Acting boldly or powerfully.

ALL-STAR GAME—The annual game that features the best players from the NHL.

ASSISTS—Passes that lead to a goal.

CHECK—A body blow that stops an opponent from advancing with the puck.

CONCUSSIONS—Head injuries that affect the brain.

CONFERENCE—A large group of teams. There are two conferences in the NHL, and each season each conference sends a team to the Stanley Cup Finals.

DISORIENTED—Confused or lost.

DIVISION—A small group of teams in a conference. Each NHL conference has three divisions.

DRAFT—The annual meeting during which NHL teams pick the top high school, college, and international players.

ENFORCER—A player whose job is to protect his teammates through physical play.

EXPANSION TEAM—A new team that joins a league already in business.

FACEOFFS—Battles for the puck that occur after play stops. Two players "face off" against each other as the referee drops the puck between them.

GENERAL MANAGER—A person who oversees all parts of a company or team.

GENERATION—A period of years roughly equal to the time it takes for a person to be born, grow up, and have children.

HALL OF FAME—The museum in Toronto, Canada, where hockey's best players are honored. A player voted into the Hall of Fame is sometimes called a "Hall of Famer."

ILL HUMOR—Another way of saying a bad mood.

INSPIRE—Give positive and confident feelings to others.

INTIMIDATION—Frightening someone into doing what you want.

JUNIOR HOCKEY—A series of leagues for players in their teens.

LINE—The trio made up by a left wing, center, and right wing.

LOGO—A symbol or design that represents a company or team.

MINOR LEAGUES—All the professional leagues that operate below the NHL.

NATIONAL HOCKEY LEAGUE (NHL)—The professional league that has been operating since 1917.

PLAYOFFS—The games played after the season to determine the league champion.

POSTSEASON—Another term for playoffs.

POWER PLAY—A game situation in which one team has at least one extra skater on the ice. A power play occurs when a player commits a penalty and is sent to the penalty box.

PROFESSIONAL—A player or team that plays a sport for money.

REVOLUTIONARY—Causing a dramatic change.

ROOKIE—A player in his first year.

SHOOTOUT—The final tiebreaker in an NHL game during the regular season. Each team picks three players to try to score one-on-one against the opposing goalie.

SHUTOUTS—Games in which a team doesn't score a goal.

STANLEY CUP—The trophy presented to the NHL champion. The first Stanley Cup was awarded in 1893.

STANLEY CUP FINALS—The final playoff series that determines the winner of the Stanley Cup.

STRATEGIES—Plans or methods for succeeding.

WEATHER FRONT—A storm or other weather conditions that move through an area.

WORLD HOCKEY ASSOCIATION (WHA)—The league that operated from 1972 to 1979.

X GAMES—An annual competition for athletes who play sports such as skateboarding and snowboarding.

LINE CHANGE

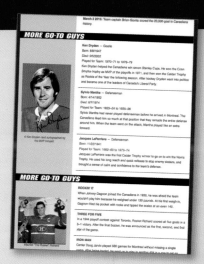

TEAM SPIRIT introduces a great way to stay up to date with your team! Visit our *LINE CHANGE* link and get connected to the latest and greatest updates. *LINE CHANGE* serves as a young reader's ticket to an exclusive web page—with more stories, fun facts, team records, and photos of the Flyers. Content is updated during and after each season. The *LINE CHANGE* feature also enables readers to send comments and letters to the author! Log onto:

www.norwoodhousepress.com/library.aspx

and click on the tab: **TEAM SPIRIT** to access *LINE CHANGE*.

Read all the books in the series to learn more about professional sports. For a complete listing of the baseball, basketball, football, and hockey teams in the **TEAM SPIRIT** series, visit our website at:

www.norwoodhousepress.com/library.aspx

ON THE ROAD

PHILADELPHIA FLYERS
3601 S. Broad Street
Philadelphia, Pennsylvania 19148-5297
(215) 465-4500
http://flyers.nhl.com

HOCKEY HALL OF FAME
Brookfield Place
30 Yonge Street
Toronto, Ontario, Canada M5E 1X8
(416) 360-7765
http://www.hhof.com

ON THE BOOKSHELF

To learn more about the sport of hockey, look for these books at your library or bookstore:

- Cameron, Steve. *Hockey Hall of Fame Treasures.* Richmond Hill, Ontario, Canada: Firefly Books, 2011.

- MacDonald, James. *Hockey Skills: How to Play Like a Pro.* Berkeley Heights, New Jersey: Enslow Elementary, 2009.

- Keltie, Thomas. *Inside Hockey! The legends, facts, and feats that made the game.* Toronto, Ontario, Canada: Maple Tree Press, 2008.

INDEX

PAGE NUMBERS IN **BOLD** REFER TO ILLUSTRATIONS.

THE TEAM

MARK STEWART has written over 200 books for kids—and more than a dozen books on hockey, including a history of the Stanley Cup and an authorized biography of goalie Martin Brodeur. He grew up in New York City during the 1960s rooting for the Rangers, but has gotten to know a couple of New Jersey Devils, so he roots for a shootout when these teams play each other. Mark comes from a family of writers. His grandfather was Sunday Editor of *The New York Times*, and his mother was Articles Editor of *Ladies' Home Journal* and *McCall's*. Mark has profiled hundreds of athletes over the past 25 years. He has also written several books about his native New York and New Jersey, his home today. Mark is a graduate of Duke University, with a degree in history. He lives and works in a home overlooking Sandy Hook, New Jersey. You can contact Mark through the Norwood House Press website.

DENIS GIBBONS is a writer and editor with *The Hockey News* and a former newsletter editor of the Toronto-based Society for International Hockey Research (SIHR). He was a contributing writer to the publication *Kings of the Ice: A History of World Hockey* and has worked as chief hockey researcher at five Winter Olympics for the ABC, CBS, and NBC television networks. Denis also has worked as a researcher for the FOX Sports Network during the Stanley Cup playoffs. He resides in Burlington, Ontario, Canada with his wife Chris.